Shapes, Shapes, Shapes

by Tana Hoban

A Mulberry Paperback Book · New York

Inquiries should be
addressed to
Greenwillow Books, a division of
William Morrow & Company, Inc.,
1350 Avenue of the Americas,
New York, New York 10019.
Printed in the United States
of America.

The Library of Congress
has cataloged the
Greenwillow Books edition of
Shapes, Shapes, Shapes
as follows:
Hoban, Tana.
Shapes, shapes, shapes.
Summary:
Photographs of familiar objects
such as chair, barrettes, and
manhole cover present a study
of rounded and angular shapes.
ISBN 0-688-05823-9
ISBN 0-688-05833-7 (lib. bdg.)
1. Geometry—Juvenile literature.
[1. Shape—Pictorial works. 2.
Geometry—Pictorial works.]
I. Title.
QA447.H63 1986
516.2'15 85-17569

10 9 8 7 6 5 4
First Mulberry Edition, 1996
ISBN 0-688-14740-2

The photographs were reproduced
from 35-mm slides and printed in full color.
The typeface is Avant Garde.

for my mother
"And all that's best of dark and bright
Meet in her aspect and her eyes."—Lord Byron

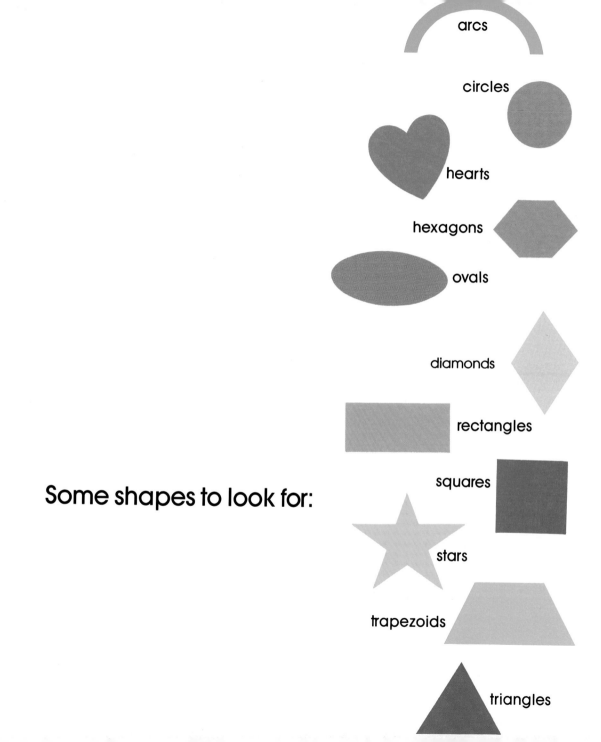

arcs

circles

hearts

hexagons

ovals

diamonds

rectangles

squares

Some shapes to look for:

stars

trapezoids

triangles